Success Strategies to BOSS UP YOUR BUSINESS

by Nadia Francois

Success Strategies to
Boss Up Your Business

by Nadia Francois

ISBN: 9798335184618

Copyright © 2024 by Heiress International Publishing

All rights reserved. No part of this book may be reproduced or transmitted in any form or by any means without written permission from the author.

Printed in the USA

Dedication

To my fellow dreamers and doers,

This book is dedicated to every woman who has ever doubted her worth, questioned her path, or faced adversity. May you find the courage to rise, the strength to persevere, and the faith to believe in God's promises for your life.

To my incredible children, who are my greatest inspiration and motivation, thank you for being my driving force and constant reminder that success is not just about achieving goals, but about creating a legacy of love and resilience.

To all the single parents navigating the challenges of entrepreneurship, may this book remind you that you are not alone and that greatness lies within you.

And to the divine power of God, whose unwavering presence and promises have guided me through every trial and triumph. This journey is a testament to His grace and faithfulness.

May "Success Strategies to Boss Up Your Business" empower you to embrace your journey, own your power, and BOSS UP in life and business.

With love and gratitude,

Nadia Francois

Table of Contents

Introduction

Chapter 1: It was All a Dream

    Strategies for Chasing Your Dreams

    Scripture Based Affirmations

Chapter 2: There's Levels to This

    Strategies for Navigating the Levels of Business

Chapter 3: Mindset Mastery

    Strategies for Mastering a Positive Mindset

Chapter 4: The Boss Up

    Strategies for Bossing Up in Business

Chapter 5: Affirmations for Bossing Up in Life and Business

Author Nadia Francois

Introduction

Welcome to Success Strategies to Boss Up Your Business, a powerful and transformative journey by Lifestyle Entrepreneur Nadia Francois. This book is more than just a guide; it is a testament to Nadia's personal evolution from a broke novice to a paid BOSS. In these pages, Nadia dives deep into her story, sharing the trials, triumphs, and invaluable lessons learned along the way.

Success is a word that means different things to different people, but for Nadia, it is about setting a goal and achieving it. As an entrepreneur and single parent, Nadia's journey is both inspiring and empowering, offering a raw and honest look at the challenges she has faced and overcome. She candidly reveals herself as a work in progress, acknowledging that through all her adversity, God's promises continue to manifest in her life.

This book is filled with Nadia's encouraging testimony, inspirational scriptures, and practical strategies designed to motivate and guide you. Whether you are looking to elevate your personal life or take your business to the next level, *Success Strategies to Boss Up Your Business* will provide you with the tools and mindset needed to achieve your goals. Get ready to be inspired, motivated, and equipped to BOSS UP in all areas of your life and business.

It Was All a Dream

Born a brown girl raised in south Louisiana, the success model was to graduate high school, attend a four-year university and work a traditional career. Well, for some reason, that was not my path. I was always a big dreamer. I dreamed of things others would say were way too big for this town and in some ways, they were right but in many more, they were dead wrong. What God has in store for my life is still in play, this is an extraordinary journey that I look forward to continuing. Being a trailblazer, innovator, visionary, or leader in any capacity requires certain qualities that we either must build upon or integrate into our lives to be successful.

My entrepreneurial journey started over 25 years ago in a time where business ownership was not popular for young black women and resources were very limited. I endured a beautiful struggle to meet the expectations of my clients, my family, and growth within my industry. It took me a while to find my target market. It took me a while to figure out systems and it took me a while to gain confidence and truly understand what I was doing. The lack of support and dream killers that I have encountered was enough to quit, but GOD!! He sustained me. He made promises to me that I had to see into fruition. My faith was tested several times, but I didn't give up, I stayed the course, and I can now be a witness to another entrepreneur that it is possible to win at this.

My business has endured a divorce, single parenting to four sons, financial lack, a recession, low self-esteem, bad business deals, illness, a pandemic and more but none of this has stopped God's purpose and plans for my business.

Some of my struggles were from bad decisions and some were destined but they are all what shaped me into the B.O.S.S. that I am today. A Bold Optimist Strategizing for Success.

Bold is defined as "showing an ability to take risks; confident and courageous." Until looking up this definition, I was misled to believe that boldness was a bad thing. When you are a born leader certain qualities cannot be hidden or denied. Boldness is a quality to be embraced and utilized strategically in business.

Walking in boldness is facing your fears and going for it. Being fearless in the face of adversity brings about success on a different level because your mind and body are in alignment for greater. Taking risks is apart of business culture and taking them on boldly is an asset to be favored. When taking risks, you are trusting your own ability, being accountable and setting a standard within your business that will be upheld and carried on throughout its legacy.

Optimist or optimism is defined as "being hopeful and confident about the future; positive." Another great quality of a born leader, optimism helps us reach our goals. More than positive thinking, optimism includes the expectancy factor. Optimistic people already expect the best outcome and if a setback occurs, they remain on course. They understand that the perception of setbacks and the response to setbacks directly impact business success. Optimism fuels business growth by exposing entrepreneurs to new ideas, boosts creativity and sparks innovation. The creating of new things and evolving in business for the present and future. Optimism is essential for business success.

Strategy is a plan of action designed to achieve a desired goal. In business, strategy is a vital component for business growth and success. As an entrepreneur, I have always operated with strategy even in in my personal life. As a single parent I had to strategize how to run my businesses, raise my babies and have room to be Nadia effectively and efficiently. It was a hard task yet achievable with faith and a plan of action, a strategy. To develop a clear strategy a few components must be considered including revenue, expenses, marketing, and competitors. A good business strategy always allows for change and growth. Some key elements that are needed in a good business strategy include a team dedicated to making the business successful, a set of effective systems that will help implement a successful business strategy, and some credible and efficient resources that can help obtain business success.

Success is defined as "obtaining wealth, prosperity, and or fame." My definition of success is one's personal journey of setting a goal and achieving it. Monetary or financial status is a good way of measuring success for some, but it ultimately comes down to personal accomplishments and self-fulfillment. Customer satisfaction and employee satisfaction also contribute to business success. Being able to help our customers solve a problem and upgrading their quality of life is a sense of accomplishment. And having good employees that are committed to your business and its values is proof of a company taking care of its employees which is also a great accomplishment. Business success can be measured in several ways and is something every entrepreneur should strive for. When God gives you a vision, He will supply the provision so go for it!! Go for it with passion, go for it with resilience and go for it in faith and it shall be done.

The smiles, the cries, the ups, the downs, the yays and the nays of entrepreneurship are all apart of the journey to soar at higher heights. It is in my experience that we walk Boldly in what God has ordained us to do being Optimistic that the goals will be achieved Strategically planned for accomplishing business Success.

Strategies for Chasing Your Dreams

As an entrepreneur who has chased her dreams and operated as a business owner for several years, I understand the journey is filled with challenges, triumphs, and invaluable lessons. The path to achieving your dreams is unique to each individual, but there are key strategies that can help you navigate this journey with confidence and determination. Here are some strategies that have guided me in achieving my entrepreneurial dreams:

Define Your Vision
Start by having a clear and compelling vision of what you want to achieve. Your vision serves as your North Star, guiding your decisions and actions. Write down your goals and break them into actionable steps. Keep revisiting your vision to stay motivated and focused on your long-term objectives.

Embrace Continuous Learning
The business world is constantly evolving, and staying ahead requires a commitment to continuous learning. Invest in your personal and professional development by attending workshops, reading books, and seeking mentorship. Staying informed about industry trends and acquiring new skills will keep you competitive and innovative.

Build a Strong Network
Surround yourself with a supportive network of mentors, peers, and advisors. Networking can open doors to new opportunities, provide valuable insights, and offer encouragement during challenging times. Cultivate relationships with people who inspire you and share your passion for entrepreneurship.

Stay Resilient
Entrepreneurship is a journey of ups and downs. Resilience is crucial for overcoming obstacles and bouncing back from setbacks. Maintain a positive mindset, learn from your failures, and adapt to changing circumstances. Remember, every challenge is an opportunity for growth and improvement.

Take Calculated Risks
Success often requires stepping out of your comfort zone and taking calculated risks. Evaluate potential opportunities and weigh the risks and rewards. Trust your instincts and be willing to take bold actions when necessary. Risk-taking is an essential part of innovation and progress.

Prioritize Self-Care
Running a business can be demanding, and it's easy to neglect your well-being. Prioritize self-care to maintain your physical, mental, and emotional health. Make time for activities that rejuvenate you, whether it's exercise, hobbies, or spending time with loved ones. A healthy and balanced lifestyle enhances your productivity and creativity.

Seek Feedback and Adjust
Feedback is a valuable tool for improvement. Seek input from customers, mentors, and peers to understand what works and what needs adjustment. Use feedback to refine your products, services, and strategies. Continuous evaluation and improvement are key to staying relevant and meeting market demands.

Stay Focused and Persistent

Achieving your dreams requires unwavering focus and persistence. Stay committed to your goals, even when faced with challenges. Keep your eyes on the prize and remind yourself of your vision. Persistence is the driving force that turns dreams into reality.

Celebrate Your Successes

Take time to celebrate your achievements, no matter how small. Recognizing your progress boosts your confidence and motivation. Celebrate milestones with your team and supporters, and use these moments as reminders of how far you've come.

Achieving your dreams as an entrepreneur is a journey that requires vision, resilience, and continuous growth. By defining your goals, embracing learning, building a strong network, staying resilient, taking risks, prioritizing self-care, seeking feedback, staying focused, and celebrating your successes, you can turn your entrepreneurial dreams into reality. Remember, you have the power to create the life and business you envision. Keep pushing forward, walking by faith, and never stop chasing your dreams.

Here are some scripture based affirmations to reference while chasing your dreams:

1. I am strong and courageous, and I trust in God's plan for me. (Joshua 1:9)

2. I can do all things through Christ who strengthens me. (Philippians 4:13)

3. God's plans for me are to prosper and not to harm me, to give me hope and a future. (Jeremiah 29:11)

4. I am fearfully and wonderfully made, equipped for every good work. (Psalm 139:14)

5. The Lord is my shepherd, I lack nothing. (Psalm 23:1)

6. I am blessed and highly favored by God. (Luke 1:28)

7. God is within me, I will not fall; He will help me at break of day. (Psalm 46:5)

8. I seek first the kingdom of God, and all these things are added to me. (Matthew 6:33)

9. I am the head and not the tail, above and not beneath. (Deuteronomy 28:13)

10. I trust in the Lord with all my heart and lean not on my own understanding. (Proverbs 3:5-6)

11. God is able to do immeasurably more than all I ask or imagine. (Ephesians 3:20)

12. The Lord directs my steps and delights in every detail of my life. (Psalm 37:23)

13. I am chosen and appointed by God to bear fruit that will last.   (John 15:16)

14. God's grace is sufficient for me, for His power is made perfect in my weakness.   (2 Corinthians 12:9)

15. I am confident of this, that He who began a good work in me will carry it on to completion. (Philippians 1:6)

16. I am more than a conqueror through Him who loves me.   (Romans 8:37)

17. God gives me wisdom generously, without finding fault.   (James 1:5)

18. I walk by faith, not by sight, trusting in God's perfect timing.   (2 Corinthians 5:7)

19. The joy of the Lord is my strength.   (Nehemiah 8:10)

20. I am rooted and grounded in love, and filled with all the fullness of God.   (Ephesians 3:17-19)

There's Levels to This

My journey through entrepreneurship is one that many women experience as they strive to fulfill their dreams of business ownership. I am sharing my story to inspire others to push through adversity no matter how dim it looks, there is a bright light at the end of the tunnel. My walk is very faith centered and in tune with God's plan for my life and I encourage anyone looking to do great things to do the same. I started in entrepreneurship at a very young age. To be honest, back then I didn't know that this would be my destiny.

At the age of 19 I started my first business, Uniforms and more. I sold medical scrubs from the trunk of my car to ladies in the healthcare industry and my fellow nursing school students. I kept it going for about 6 or 7 months until my inventory ran out and I couldn't afford to replenish my stock. As a novice entrepreneur, this season taught me the importance of investing into my business, good record keeping and audience targeting. At that time, I was also a broke college student pursuing a nursing degree, so the business idea was on point, but I didn't have the knowledge or direction I needed to fully see this business idea into fruition. Sometimes we can enter a situation prematurely or without proper preparation and it does not end as planned.

As life progressed and I began maturing into an adult life brought about a lot of trials and test that I was not prepared for. Now this was at a time in history where there was no google or web assistance we barely had computers so I literally had to teach myself how to overcome my business struggles or fail forward.

In my junior year of college I received the news that I was expecting twin boys, a bitter sweet moment because my plans of becoming a nurse were put on hold but for a wonderful reason. I never thought that I would be a mother, let alone to twins but, I embraced it and looked forward to the birth of my little men. Three months after giving birth to the twins I was married with a brand new perspective on life, new goals, and new aspirations to look forward to. Shortly after the wedding I found out I was pregnant again. This was devastating to me because I already had two babies and was suffering from post partum depression. My twins were born prematurely and had to remain in the NICU for 4 weeks after their birth, so that separation took a toll on my mental status. Thoughts of the addition of another baby were very overwhelming and had me wondering how would we make it when my husband was working a mediocre job and I had not finished school.

As an only child and pretty much a loner, God and I already had a special relationship. So, I prayed and sought counsel from my Father and He told me, "everything that you need is already in your hands." I struggled with this for a while then I realized what He meant. In my early teens I would style hair from my mother's kitchen. It was mainly my friends and family but they were all satisfied and it paid well. Thinking back on what started as a hustle, God was telling me to use my talents. So I began to research cosmetology schools in my area and stared applying to them. Confirmation of this decision came when I was accepted into a school and also given a full scholarship from the local JTPA program. Schooling pain in full!

I committed to studying, practicing and passing my state board exams and not only did I graduate and pass my licensing exams, I earned my barber license as well. I opened my own barber salon and business was booming. A true testament of God's grace and mercy.

Shortly after opening my salon my family life had fallen a part. My husband wasn't keeping the vows. I had dealt with infidelity issues in the past but at this point in my life, it was completely unacceptable. It was important for me to feel safe and supported in my relationships and at this point, I wasn't feeling either. I soon confronted him and we split up shortly after. It was a hard blow. He abandoned us physically, emotionally, and financially. I suddenly became a single mom. Talk about a swift transition. At this point I had four sons, the twins were 6, my middle son was 5 and my baby boy was one year old.

I was now the mommy, the daddy, the bread winner and the baby sitter, but GOD had positioned me right where I needed to be. I felt like such a failure because my relationship was over and I had to raise the boys alone. I went into deep prayer mode searching for peace and understanding. It was right there where I learned about grief and loss and that no one had to physically die for me to feel this way. So naturally, I began going through those phases of grief and experiencing depression, guilt and shame. I sat with my self and reflected on my life as a wife, mother, entrepreneur, and daughter and I realized that I had been living my life to please others and not myself. I was stressed out, unhappy, my self esteem had hit rock bottom and I was holding on by a thread mentally.

After a few years of self destructing behavior, trying to drown the pain, I had lost a lot of my clients and friends. I did not care who I hurt because I was hurt. I went through so much grief and anger, this was a very emotional time in my life. So of course, I had to have my occasional talk with God and He told me to focus on living my life and raising my kids pleasing to Him and He would do the rest, and that's just what I began to do. At this time, I also committed to renewing my faith and living a kingdom lifestyle.

I took my kids to church, prayed over them and if I couldn't go, I sent them with others. I was running my business and taking care of my kids all on my own. The beautiful part of this level of my life was that even though I felt like a failure, God had positioned me to WIN! Being a salon owner, I was able to bring my kids to work with me if I had to, leave to attend their school programs and extra-curricular activities, and maintain my clientele to keep the funds rolling in. God was definitely doing his part. When I lacked, my family stepped up to help me in any way that they could. We received no child support or visits from their father for many years. My hands were actually taking care of us!! God was keeping His promise so I had to keep mine.

Even though entrepreneurship brings a lot of freedom it also brings about more bills and unexpected expenses. The struggle was so real, there were times where I couldn't do anything leisure unless someone treated me. Some days we lived off noodles and cereal but we were never hungry or in the dark and this was something to be grateful for. During this time, I learned resilience, discipline and my faith walk was strengthened. My relationship with God was growing and my perspective on life began to change.

My salon business boomed for about 5 or 6 years, then the recession hit. Business slowed down to nothing swiftly and I was once again forced to enter the workforce. Of course I was very reluctant but I had to do what was best for my family. I was blessed to be able to work in my industry at a local cosmetology school as an administrator. With previous experience as an office assistant, excellent organization skills and the forward thinking mindset I possessed this was a great position for me to excel and build my resume.

Accepting this position, along with my struggles in the salon inspired me to go back to school and pursue my Batchelor's degree in Business Administration. I wanted to know all I could about starting, running, and maintaining a successful business. This was around 2009 and the emergence of technology and the need for continuing education was required for the level up. The boys were growing up yet still very needy so being employed actually helped bring some structure along with a steady income. I was employed at the school for a little over a year then I was back to being a full time entrepreneur.

During my employment at the school I learned so much of what and what not to do in business. I also learned about the heart and keeping it out of your business and employment decisions. Our feelings can make us very vulnerable and susceptible to works of the enemy. The two greatest lessons from this experience were 1.) Don't break your won rules and 2.) Don't do business in your feelings. I also learned that when dealing with the federal government in any form of business, to do the right thing. Do no take any shortcuts and operate in integrity in all areas of life.

This time I looked forward to being fully self employed again, especially being enrolled in business school. I was able to implement the things I learned in school into my own business. I also realized that a background in business was very beneficial to a beauty business. The scope of business that is taught in cosmetology school is not thorough enough for novice business owners and in this industry we graduate as business owners.

Over the years I have had plenty of side hustles and hobbies, but I was now equipped to own and manage successful businesses. I have always considered myself a born entrepreneur because I have always had a grind and hustle that was unmatched and I believe that no one else should benefit from this favor other than God. Many people have tried to use me for my gift and it just never works out for them. God has a way of protecting us from the scoundrels even when the scales are still on our eyes. New levels bring new devils. But God!

My journey to becoming a serial entrepreneur began in my salon. I truly believed that I needed an income for each person that I was supporting so I added products and services that would boost my revenue. Holding on to my beliefs, God promised me that I would still have the desires of my heart and I would not have to stress, worry, or wonder how. By this time, I had recently graduated in my degree program. So I began to re-evaluate my life and business to determine what I wanted for my future and it became very clear that I was to use my knowledge to help others build successful businesses. I had been giving out free advice and helping others for years so it was inevitable that I get paid to do it. So I started professionally consulting small businesses on start-up and business development. My passion for the beauty industry inspired me to start contributing my business knowledge to the beauty industry. I have always loved my industry and the way that it raised me, so I created a tool to help others. The Entrepreneur Activity Workbook was published in 2017 and assists business owners in the planning stages of their business guiding them through the steps of creating a plan and ultimately producing a working business plan for their business.

I was also blessed to educate my fellow beauty professionals on business at industry conferences and hair shows. As I further matured in business, I was blessed to open and operate businesses for myself and others as a Business Strategist and Consultant. Still using my talents, I was able to provide for my four sons as they graduated high school and grew into responsible young men.

My sons helped me with many of my businesses and were able to see what hard work, sacrifice, and faith can produce. My success story is still being written, but God has definitely carried me through many seasons as an entrepreneur. I am encouraged to share about my journey as a single parent in entrepreneurship the most because many women can't see past motherhood to grow their businesses into generational wealth. I encourage any woman that is aspiring to be a business owner to keep going, trust God and walk in His promises. Life has a way of going on, but we must show up everyday for our family and our businesses. The stretching is only a test that ultimately bring us to our testimony. God is amazing and has the best stored up for the members of His Kingdom. Grace and mercy are our portion and never giving up is the key to unlocking the doors of adversity.

Here are some of my favorite Bible verses that helped to keep me on track and focused on God's promises for my life and overcoming my struggles:

Jeremiah 29:11(NIV)," For I know the plans I have for you," declares the Lord, plans to prosper you and not to harm you, plans to give you hope and a future."

This scripture tells me that while in my mother's wound, there was a purpose for my life. God put me here for a reason and everything that I go through is a part of His purpose, not to harm me, and that the blessing is in the lesson. We all have trials and tribulations in our lives but those are necessary to mold us into the person God wants us to be. Gracefully broken...

Isaiah 43:2 (NIV), "When you pass through the waters, I will be with you and when you pass through them, they will not sweep over you. When you walk through the fire, you will not be burned; the flames will not set you ablaze."

This scripture tells me that God has me no matter what I'm going through. Sometimes we get caught up in the what and forget about the why. There is a reason that we go through what we go through that's why it is important to stay focused on God.

Isaiah 54:17(NKJV), "No weapon formed against you shall prosper, And every tongue which rises against you in judgment You shall condemn. This is the heritage of the servants of the Lord, And their righteousness is from Me' says the Lord."

This scripture tells me that any negative or evil thing that comes my way is already defeated. That judgment does not belong to man, but God.

1 John 1:9(NKJV), "But if we confess our sins to him, he is faithful and just to forgive us our sins and cleanse us from all wickedness."

This scripture tells me that I am forgiven for all the sins I have committed. All I have to do is confess and ask God to forgive me and I will have a fresh start. God is a forgiving God and everyday is a new day.

Deuteronomy 31:8(NKJV), "And the Lord, He is the one who goes before you. He will be with you, He will not leave you nor forsake you, do not fear or be dismayed."

This scripture tells me to not be afraid to go after what I want in life because God has already made a way for me to achieve it and he will be with me along the way."

As an entrepreneur, the journey to business success is both challenging and rewarding. It involves navigating through different levels, each with its unique hurdles and milestones. It is my prayer that anyone that reads my story understands that Faith, Resilience, Consistency, Commitment, and Focus will lead to a successful business. There will be seasons of shortfalls and setbacks, but when you keep your purpose and God's plan at the forefront, YOU WILL WIN!!

Strategies for Navigating the Levels of Business Success

Level 1: Startup Phase

The startup phase is about turning your idea into reality. During this stage, focus on:

1. Solidifying Your Vision: Clearly define your business vision, mission, and goals. A strong foundation will guide your decisions and actions.

2. Market Research: Conduct thorough market research to understand your target audience, competitors, and industry trends. This information will help you create a product or service that meets market needs.

3. Business Plan: Develop a detailed business plan outlining your strategy, financial projections, and marketing approach. This plan will serve as a roadmap for your business and attract potential investors.

4. Networking: Build a network of mentors, advisors, and peers. Their insights and support can be invaluable as you navigate the startup phase.

Level 2: Growth Phase

Once your business is up and running, the focus shifts to growth and scaling. Key strategies include:

1. Refining Operations: Streamline your operations to improve efficiency and productivity. Implement systems and processes that can scale with your business.

2. Marketing and Branding: Invest in marketing and branding to increase visibility and attract more customers. Utilize digital marketing, social media, and other platforms to boost awareness of your business.

3. Customer Focus: Prioritize customer satisfaction and retention. Collect feedback, address concerns promptly, and continuously improve your products or services based on customer needs.

4. Financial Management: Monitor your finances closely. Ensure you have a healthy cash flow, manage expenses, and plan for future investments.

Level 3: Maturity Phase

In the maturity phase, your business is stable, and the focus is on sustaining success and exploring new opportunities. Strategies for this stage include:

1. Innovation: Continuously innovate to stay ahead of competitors and meet evolving market demands. Explore new product lines, services, or business models.

2. Diversification: Diversify your offerings or enter new markets to reduce risk and create additional revenue streams.

3. Leadership Development: Invest in developing your leadership skills and building a strong management team. Empower your team to take on more responsibilities and drive the business forward.

4. Community Engagement: Build a strong brand reputation by engaging with your community and giving back. Corporate social responsibility initiatives can enhance your brand image and customer loyalty.

Level 4: Expansion Phase

In the expansion phase, you look to scale your business further and potentially enter new markets. Key strategies include:

1. Market Research: Conduct comprehensive market research to identify new opportunities and understand the nuances of different markets.

2. Strategic Partnerships: Form strategic partnerships and alliances to expand your reach and capabilities. Collaborate with other businesses to leverage their strengths and resources.

3. Investment: Seek additional funding or investment to support your expansion plans. Present a compelling case to investors by showcasing your growth potential and track record.

4. Global Reach: Consider expanding your business internationally. Adapt your products, services, and marketing strategies to suit local markets.

Level 5: Legacy Phase

At this stage, your focus shifts to leaving a lasting legacy and ensuring the sustainability of your business. Strategies for this phase include:

1. Succession Planning: Develop a succession plan to ensure a smooth transition of leadership. Identify and mentor future leaders within your organization.

2. Sustainable Practices: Implement sustainable business practices that contribute to long-term success and positively impact the environment and society.

3. Mentorship: Give back by mentoring other entrepreneurs and sharing your knowledge and experiences. Your insights can help others navigate their entrepreneurial journeys.

4. Continuous Learning: Stay curious and committed to learning. Keep abreast of industry trends, technological advancements, and emerging opportunities.

Progressing through the levels of business success requires strategic planning, adaptability, and a commitment to continuous improvement. By implementing these strategies, you can navigate the entrepreneurial journey with confidence and achieve lasting success. Remember, every challenge is an opportunity to grow, and every milestone is a testament to your resilience and determination.

Mindset Mastery

During my entrepreneurship journey, I often fought against negative thoughts, naysayers and disbelief that my dreams were attainable. It wasn't until I reached a certain point in life where all I could do was look to our Father God and allow Him to order my steps into my purpose and ultimately reveal my destiny. The word destiny had never crossed my mind. But when I made the decision to give my life to Christ, my destiny was revealed.

God had a purpose and plan for my life when I was in my mother's womb. I had to take the time to discover who I was and who I belonged to, my mindset had to be adjusted to a kingdom mindset with kingdom expectations, and I had to activate my faith. These actions were my investments into my destiny. We must deposit intentional investments daily to ensure a positive mindset and to fuel our destiny.

There were a few scriptures I meditated on daily in order to make this shift:

1. "For I know the thoughts that I think toward you, says the Lord, thoughts of peace and not of evil, to give you a future and a hope." Jeremiah 29:11 (NKJV)

2. "I will praise You, for I am fearfully and wonderfully made; Marvelous are Your works,
And that my soul knows very well." Psalms 139:14 (NKJV)

3. "I can do all things through Christ who strengthens me." Philippians 4:13 (NKJV)

Once my mindset was adjusted, I then had to heal. Every issue that affected my growth had to be resolved. I had to forgive some people with no apology, I had to end some relationships with no explanation, and I also had to forgive myself for the bad decisions and trauma I put myself through.

A true healing, a thorough healing because in order to walk into my destiny all the dead weight had to be shed. This healing brought about a fresh feeling, a feeling of newness, peace, and a burst of confidence. I finally knew my worth, I finally knew my value and the value of being associated with me as well. I was able to determine what was good for me and what wasn't, who was for me and who wasn't and most of all I loved me and recognized my true worth. There was no more room for mediocrity in my life. I was forced to level up in every area of my life and claim my keys to the kingdom, continuing to invest in my success.

This mindset shift also required me to understand that life is not meant to be an easy road but a learning experience that brings us closer to God. The struggles that we face are not meant to break us but to strengthen us for what's to come. God has promised us the desires of our heart however He didn't promise that it would be an easy task. Trials and tribulations will come we just have to faith our way through.

Walking in faith means looking at our experiences from a heavenly perspective rather than an earthly perspective. Knowing that if God has pulled you through once, He will do it again and remembering that we walk by faith and not by sight. Sometimes things can look dim in the natural, but God can turn it around for our good. Investing positive thoughts and actions into these experiences will produce a heavenly outcome. There are some daily activities that can be very helpful in maintaining a positive and productive mindset:

1. Prayer/ Meditation
Prayer and mediation are excellent ways of getting closer to God, reducing anxiety and stress levels, increasing self-awareness, and helping make better decisions.

2. Affirmations
Affirmations help disrupt negative thinking, boost our mood, boosts confidence and self-esteem, lowers stress and help build us up in difficult situations.

3. Focus on Positive Solutions
Focusing on positive solutions allows us to maintain a positive attitude, be more alert, work better with others, reduce stress, and boost immunity.

4. Journaling
Journaling helps with self-discovery, understanding triggers, working through conflict, and managing growth.

5. Self-care
Having a consistent self-care routine has been proven to increase happiness, improve physical health, boost self-esteem, reduce stress and anxiety, and increases energy.

6. Environment Change
Changing your environment makes it easier to do the right thing. If we are not surrounded by negativity, then it's easier to make better decisions and maintain a positive attitude.

The steps that I took in order to heal, forgive, and focus all directly affected me in determining my true purpose in life. Gaining that personal relationship with God tied everything together. He truly directs my path and orders my steps along the path. He is my guiding light when there are no answers. I look at the steps towards my purpose as an investment into my success. There is a certain level of work that we have to put in to have a truly happy, favored, and blessed life.

As an entrepreneur, one of the most crucial aspects of your journey is developing a mindset that not only believes in your potential for success but actively cultivates it. Transitioning from self-doubt to self-assuredness takes deliberate effort and strategic thinking. Mastering the mindset of business success is a continuous journey of growth and self-improvement. Remember, success starts in your mind—believe in yourself, and watch your business flourish.

Strategies for Mastering a Positive Mindset

1. Embrace a Growth Mindset
A growth mindset, coined by psychologist Carol Dweck, is the belief that abilities and intelligence can be developed with effort, learning, and persistence. Embrace challenges as opportunities to learn rather than as obstacles. Celebrate your progress, no matter how small, and view failures as stepping stones to success.

2. Set Clear, Achievable Goals
Having clear, well-defined goals gives you a roadmap for your business journey. Break down larger goals into smaller, actionable steps to avoid feeling overwhelmed. Regularly review and adjust your goals to stay on track and maintain momentum.

3. Visualize Success
Visualization is a powerful tool for building confidence and clarity. Spend a few minutes each day picturing yourself achieving your business goals. Imagine the details: the way it feels, looks, and even sounds. This practice can help reinforce your belief in your ability to succeed.

4. Surround Yourself with Positivity
The people you surround yourself with have a significant impact on your mindset. Build a network of supportive, like-minded individuals who encourage and inspire you. Avoid naysayers and negative influences that can drain your motivation and self-belief.

5. Invest in Continuous Learning
Stay curious and committed to learning. Attend workshops, read books, take courses, and seek out mentors who can provide guidance and insights.

Continuous learning helps you stay adaptable and open to new ideas, keeping your mindset fresh and innovative.

6. Practice Self-Compassion
Entrepreneurship is a demanding journey, and it's essential to be kind to yourself. Acknowledge your efforts, forgive your mistakes, and give yourself credit for your accomplishments. Self-compassion helps maintain a positive and resilient mindset, especially during tough times.

7. Develop a Daily Routine
A structured daily routine can enhance productivity and focus. Start your day with activities that set a positive tone, such as exercise, meditation, or journaling. Establish work habits that keep you organized and efficient, reducing stress and increasing your sense of control.

8. Stay Flexible and Adaptable
The business landscape is constantly changing, and flexibility is key to staying relevant and successful. Be willing to pivot and adapt your strategies as needed. An adaptable mindset allows you to embrace change and seize new opportunities as they arise.

9. Celebrate Milestones
Take time to celebrate your achievements, both big and small. Recognizing your progress boosts morale and motivation. It also reinforces the positive belief that you are moving in the right direction and achieving your business goals.

10. Focus on Your Why
Remember why you started your entrepreneurial

journey in the first place. Keep your purpose and passion at the forefront of your mind. When you stay connected to your "why," it fuels your determination and helps you push through challenges with renewed vigor.

The Boss Up

Starting a business is a huge leap of faith and financial risk that is sometimes frightening for a new entrepreneur. Having a background of over 25 years of building my business in the hair care industry and over 15 years of consulting, I have learned that this journey is not for the weak or faint at heart. If you give up easy, this is not for you.

Entrepreneurship is a lot of hard work and sacrifice. But on the other hand, it is one of the most rewarding occupations one can ever have. The freedom alone is what is most valuable to me. As a single parent to four sons that I have raised on my entrepreneur's salary for the past 18 years, we have not missed a beat. So, to achieve the income required to maintain my household as a single parent, I had to BOSS UP!!

I bossed up in every area of my life including my spiritual life. I made a decision to put God first in life and business and this was a game changer. I then became very discipline with my time, energy, and resources being more intentional with my business moves. I developed a strategy to help me generate an income that can always be increased with more effort yet sustainable when life happens. I discovered that key to building a successful business required some essential elements no matter what industry or field.

This book is book is a small excerpt of my journey as a business owner and contains several strategies to assist other business owners along their journey. My faith plays the largest part in my success. Without God on my side and in my heart I would not be where I am today. My charge to any reader of this book is to trust God. Put your business in His hands and you will not fail.

Strategies for Bossing Up in Life & Business

Set Clear Goals and Celebrate Achievements
Define specific, measurable business goals. Celebrate every milestone reached, no matter how small, to build confidence and recognize progress.

Invest in Personal Development
Attend workshops, seminars, and conferences to enhance your skills and knowledge. Personal growth leads to professional confidence.

Seek Mentorship and Coaching
Connect with mentors or business coaches who can offer guidance, support, and encouragement. Learning from others' experiences can provide valuable insights and boost self-assurance.

Cultivate a Strong Support Network
Surround yourself with positive, supportive individuals who encourage your growth and success. Networking with other businesswomen can provide inspiration and a sense of community.

Practice Self-Compassion
Acknowledge your accomplishments and be kind to yourself. Understand that setbacks are part of the journey and use them as learning experiences.

Upgrade Your Online Presence
Ensure your website is up-to-date, user-friendly, and mobile-optimized. An engaging, professional website is essential for attracting and retaining customers.

Leverage Social Media
Use social media platforms to engage with your audience, share your brand story, and promote your products or services. Consistent and authentic content can enhance your brand's visibility and customer loyalty.

Utilize Digital Marketing Tools
Invest in tools like email marketing software, CRM systems, and analytics platforms. These tools can help streamline your marketing efforts, track customer behavior, and optimize your sales funnel.

Embrace E-commerce
If applicable, expand your business into the online marketplace. Selling products or services online can reach a broader audience and increase sales.

Explore Automation and AI
Consider using automation tools and artificial intelligence to streamline operations, improve customer service, and enhance productivity. Chatbots, automated email campaigns, and AI-driven analytics can save time and resources.

Diversify Revenue Streams
Explore new products, services, or markets to diversify your income sources. This can include offering digital products, online courses, or subscription-based services.

Enhance Customer Experience
Focus on delivering exceptional customer service. Happy customers are more likely to become repeat buyers and refer others, boosting sales through word-of-mouth.

Implement Pricing Strategies

Reevaluate your pricing model to ensure it's competitive and reflects the value you provide. Consider offering tiered pricing, bundled packages, or loyalty programs to encourage more sales.

Increase Online Visibility

Invest in search engine optimization (SEO) and paid advertising to increase your online visibility. The more visible your business, the more potential customers you can attract.

Analyze and Optimize Financials

Regularly review your financial statements to identify areas where you can reduce costs and increase profits. Focus on high-margin products or services and consider renegotiating contracts with suppliers.

Continuous Learning

Stay updated on industry trends, technological advancements, and market demands. Being informed can help you make strategic decisions and stay ahead of the competition.

Time Management

Prioritize tasks and delegate where possible. Efficient time management allows you to focus on high-impact activities that drive business growth.

Self-Care

Take care of your physical and mental health. A well-balanced lifestyle boosts productivity and enables you to handle business challenges with a clear mind.

Here's a list of free business apps and resources that small business owners can utilize to streamline operations, boost productivity, and enhance their businesses:

Productivity and Project Management
1. Trello - A visual project management tool that helps you organize tasks and projects using boards, lists, and cards.
2. Asana - A project management tool that allows teams to collaborate, manage tasks, and track progress.
3. Slack - A messaging app for teams that facilitates communication and collaboration.
4. Google Workspace - Includes free tools like Google Docs, Sheets, and Slides for document creation and collaboration, as well as Google Calendar for scheduling.
5. Notion- An all-in-one workspace for note-taking, project management, and collaboration.

Financial Management
1. Wave - Free accounting software that includes invoicing, accounting, and receipt scanning.
2. Mint - A personal finance and budgeting tool that can also be used for tracking small business expenses.
3. QuickBooks Online - While typically a paid service, QuickBooks offers a free trial for tracking expenses and managing financials.
4. Square Register -Free financial management platform with credit card processing and invoicing capabilities.

Marketing and Social Media
1. Canva - A graphic design tool with free templates for creating social media posts, marketing materials, and more.

2. Buffer - A social media management tool that allows you to schedule posts and analyze their performance.
3. Hootsuite - Another social media management platform that offers free scheduling and monitoring for multiple accounts.
4. Mailchimp - An email marketing service with free plans for creating and managing email campaigns.

Website and Online Presence
1. WordPress - A free content management system for building and managing websites and blogs.
2. Wix - Offers a free plan for creating a website with drag-and-drop tools.
3. Google My Business - A free tool to manage your business's online presence across Google, including Search and Maps.

Customer Relationship Management (CRM)
1. HubSpot CRM - A free CRM tool that helps manage customer relationships, track interactions, and streamline sales processes.
2. Zoho CRM - Offers a free plan for managing customer relationships and sales pipelines.

Communication and Virtual Meetings
1. Zoom - A video conferencing tool that offers free meetings with basic features.
2. Skype - A communication tool for free voice and video calls, instant messaging, and file sharing.

File Storage and Sharing
1. Google Drive - Provides free cloud storage for documents, photos, and other files.
2. Dropbox - Offers free cloud storage and file sharing for easy access to business documents.

Analytics and SEO
1. Google Analytics - A free tool for tracking and analyzing website traffic and user behavior.
2. Ubersuggest - A free SEO tool for keyword research and competitor analysis.

Legal and Compliance
1. Rocket Lawyer - Offers free legal documents and contracts with a trial period.
2. DocuSign - Provides a free trial for electronic signatures and document management.

Time Management
1. Toggl - A time-tracking tool that helps you monitor how much time you spend on different tasks and projects.
2. RescueTime - A tool that tracks your digital activity to help you understand and improve your productivity.

Affirmations to Boss Up Your Life & Business

1. I have the courage to pursue my dreams fearlessly.
2. I am capable of achieving anything I set my mind to.
3. My dreams are valid, and I am worthy of pursuing them.
4. I trust in my abilities and believe in my vision.
5. I am determined and focused on making my dreams a reality.
6. I deserve to live a life that fulfills me and brings me joy.
7. Every step I take brings me closer to my goals.
8. I am not afraid of challenges; they are opportunities for growth.
9. I release all doubts and embrace my limitless potential.
10. I have the strength and resilience to overcome any obstacle.
11. I am bold, brave, and unstoppable in the pursuit of my dreams.
12. I am constantly evolving and improving on my journey to success.
13. I am worthy of success and the life I envision.
14. I attract opportunities that align with my passions and goals.
15. I believe in my dreams, and I take action to make them come true.
16. I am surrounded by supportive people who encourage my growth.

17. I am creative and resourceful in finding ways to achieve my dreams.
18. I honor my passions by pursuing them with dedication and enthusiasm.
19. I am in control of my destiny and make choices that lead to my success.
20. I am confident in my path and trust the process of achieving my dreams.
21. I am committed to my personal growth and success.
22. I am capable of achieving greatness in all areas of my life.
23. I embrace challenges as opportunities for growth and learning.
24. I deserve to live a life filled with abundance and joy."
25. I am constantly evolving and becoming the best version of myself.
26. I am confident in my ability to overcome obstacles and achieve my goals.
27. I have the power to create the life I desire.
28. I am worthy of reaching my highest potential.
29. I am open to new opportunities and experiences that elevate my life.
30. I trust in my journey and have faith in my future.
31. I release any limiting beliefs and embrace my limitless potential.
32. I am fearless in the pursuit of my dreams and aspirations.

33. I choose to focus on the good in every situation.
33. I am capable of transforming my thoughts and my life.
34. I radiate positivity and attract positive experiences.
35. I am in control of my thoughts and emotions.
36. I believe in my ability to create a joyful and fulfilling life.
37. I choose to see the best in myself and others.
38. I am grateful for the blessings and opportunities in my life.
39. I let go of negativity and embrace positivity.
40. I trust that everything is unfolding for my highest good.
41. I am resilient, and I bounce back from setbacks stronger than before.
42. I am worthy of happiness, love, and success.
43. I am at peace with myself and the world around me.
44. I focus on solutions rather than problems.
45. I am grateful for the lessons and growth that challenges bring.
46. I choose to cultivate a mindset of abundance and joy.
47. I am surrounded by love, peace, and positive energy.
48. I am open to new perspectives and possibilities.

49. I attract positivity and joy into my life every day.
50. I am kind to myself and speak to myself with love and compassion.
51. I am confident, strong, and capable of achieving my dreams.
52. I am a confident and capable leader in my business.
53. I am the CEO of my life and my business, and I make decisions with clarity and purpose.
54. I am worthy of success, wealth, and recognition in my field.
55. I have the skills and knowledge to run a successful business.
56. I am constantly growing and evolving as a business leader.
57. I attract opportunities that align with my business goals and values.
58. I am fearless in pursuing my business vision and dreams.
59. I am surrounded by a strong network of support and resources.
60. I handle challenges with grace and turn them into opportunities for growth.
61. I trust in my ability to create a thriving and prosperous business.
62. I am a master at balancing creativity and strategy in my business endeavors.
63. I am confident in my ability to make smart and profitable decisions.

64. I am resilient, and I bounce back from setbacks stronger and wiser.

65. I am dedicated to providing exceptional value and service to my clients.

66. I deserve to be paid well for the expertise and value I bring.

67. I am an inspiration to other women entrepreneurs.

68. I embrace innovation and am always open to new ideas and strategies.

69. I am focused, disciplined, and committed to achieving my business goals.

70. I am proud of the business I am building and the impact it has.

71. I am a powerful, unstoppable force in the business world.

These affirmations are designed to boost confidence, foster a strong mindset, and encourage women to take bold, decisive actions in their business ventures. Repeating these affirmations can help instill a sense of empowerment and purpose. BOSS UP!!

Order the Boss Up Your Business CEO Planner for step-by-step guidance on starting and growing your business.

SCAN TO ORDER

Author Nadia Francois

Nadia Francois Bio

Nadia Francois is a lifestyle entrepreneur with a heart for people. Business Strategist, Author, Media Maven and a Hairstylist by trade, Nadia holds current licenses in Cosmetology and Barbering, a B.S. in Business Administration along with several certifications. The Louisiana native began her entrepreneurial journey at the age of 19 and has used her experiences and knowledge to help other business owners start and grow their ventures for over 25 years. Nadia continues to thrive and expand in her beauty endeavors, Heiress Haircare Systems and Heiress Beauty Lounge which she describes as her passion because "boosting a person's confidence is a different level of accomplishment."

Nadia continues to add to her beauty legacy by serving as an educator in the industry where she helps industry professionals BOSS UP their businesses with proven strategies to increase their income. She has graced classrooms in Georgia, Texas, and Louisiana blazing trails in the industry providing her published workbooks, planners, and e-books as tools of the trade. In 2022, Nadia was awarded the "Game Changer" award by the Beauty Industry Community Awards Organization. In 2023 Nadia began her journey as a Cranial Prosthesis Specialist and has now entered the medical hair loss industry.

Nadia also serves as a mentor to female business owners and single mothers. She uses her life experiences and the outreach of other mentors and professionals to empower our women, children and entrepreneurs to become successful, confident, self-sufficient members of society. She is also the Founder and Executive Director of

Sistars of Empowerment, Inc. a nonprofit that focuses on empowering, educating, and inspiring women and mentoring the youth in the community. In 2013, she decided to pursue her dream of giving back to the community and established a platform that provides tools for enhancing knowledge, life, and personal development skills. SOE is a growing sisterhood that incorporates motivational and business workshops, youth confidence and esteem sessions, and mentorship. SOE has even received a proclamation from the city and commendation from the state for its community involvement and Women's Empowerment Week which takes place annually during Women's History Month and Domestic Violence Education Week every October.

The organization continues to give back to the community throughout the year with its youth scholarship program for high school graduates, teen summit and other outreach events. SOE also serves a community of women and single mothers through their women's mentorship program, EvolveHer. Where SOE mentors women in the local housing authority communities to enhance mindsets and shift perspectives.

In 2018, Nadia served as the inaugural Ms. Black Louisiana Empowerment representing her state by serving at several community projects and hosting outreach activities that contributed to the advancement of women and youth in the community. In 2018, Nadia also attained recognition as International Best Selling Author for Better Woman Better World Book One. In 2019, she was nominated for Business Woman of the Year by the Greater Southwest Louisiana Black Chamber of Commerce.

In 2020, Nadia became Visionary Author for her own faith-based compilation, What's Your Super Power anthology where this woman of faith along with an amazing group of female authors contributed their compelling and captivating stories of strength and resilience while overcoming life's obstacles. Nadia also published the What's your Super Power Reflection Journal and Power Notes free writing journal as companions to help women discover their God given super power.

In December 2020, this trailblazer stepped out on faith and became the host of What's Your Super Power TV (WYSP TV), which is currently streamed via YouTube. Nadia interviews powerhouse women, spotlights minority business owners, and introduces community leaders to her audience. In 2021, Nadia continued to enhance her digital footprint with the addition of Power Conversations Magazine & Podcast which are additional extensions of her digital media empire that caters to entrepreneurs and their advancement. For her outstanding work in the media, she was honored the Bosses & Bossettas Platinum Award in 2022. Nadia is also the host and curator of the International Author Boss Awards founded in 2020.

Nadia is a publisher, contributing author and visionary author of several international best-selling titles and was nominated for a Distinguished Author's Guild Award in 2023. She hosts several development events for authors including the annual Author Boss Book Festival. Nadia has spoken on various global platforms and has launched her signature coaching program Boss Up Your Business Coaching and her Boss Up Your Business CEO Planner where she assists the busy entrepreneur in streamlining her processes and procedures through organization, time management, and automation which ultimately result in more flexibility and increased profits. Nadia believes in working smarter and not harder even with multiple streams flowing.

This goal-getter contributes her success to grace and mercy. Her number one assignment is being the mother and sole provider for her four sons, the driving force behind her persistent hustle and diligent pursuit of greatness.

Connect with Nadia at www.nadiafrancois.com

Book a consultation at www.meetwithheiress.com

SCAN TO CONNECT

NOTES

NOTES

NOTES

NOTES

NOTES

NOTES

NOTES

NOTES

NOTES

NOTES

NOTES

Heiress International Publishing

"WE CAN MAKE YOUR PUBLISHING DREAMS A REALITY"

Now Accepting New Clients

Solo Book Projects
Anthology Projects
Magazines
E-Books

Cover to Cover | Cover to Launch | Ghost Publishing

Call For Info
225-681-3530

Email us at
info@heiressbooks.com

Visit Our Site
WWW.HEIRESSBOOKS.COM/BOOKS

www.ingramcontent.com/pod-product-compliance
Lightning Source LLC
Chambersburg PA
CBHW072018230526
45479CB00008B/275